The Garden

our inner seasons
of
planting and growth

The Seventh Elm
P.O. Box 2905 Fargo, ND
58108

The Garden

Our Inner Seasons of Planting and Growth

By Donna Kavanaugh
and
Helen Bjornson

Illustrations by Virginia Janousek

First Printing December 1993

Second Printing September 1995

The Seventh Elm P.O. Box 2905 Fargo, ND 58108

This little book came about
because two friends got together
and their hearts started writing.

It is dedicated to all those we love
and take into our inner gardens
. . . . and to all those we will love
and meet there in the future.

The Garden

Contents

Virginia Janousek   Garden's Harvest   oil   22x28″

The Garden

PART I
Donna Kavanaugh

A garden! There's nothing in the world that holds the mystery of life like a garden. It can be large as a park or as small as a patio planter. The size doesn't effect the dimensions of the dream.

We escape the monotony of the barren season with the creation of mental images for the coming growing season. These pictures in our mind's photo album are enhanced by browsing through the seed catalogs and gardening books.

When the garden is finally planted and the dreams take on reality, nothing prepares us for the miracle. We watch with wonder as that seasonal splendor arises from the tiny seeds and frail plants we carefully placed in the soil. Each year we ponder again the mystery and unseen power of it all.

Our spiritual yard is no different from our back yard. We can never fully contain the joy that comes when those tiny seeds and frail plants of faith and hope burst into the splendor of inner growth, strength and love. We endured the barren season and held on to our dreams. The inner miracle has happened! We survived.

We come to understand that the process of inner gardening contains many miracles. We learn to take care not to miss them.

We learn to take care not to miss life.

Beginning

A garden begins in the heart and mind. Little by little we put a picture together of the site and pattern of the flower beds. This period of quiet creating is a very special one. The snow may still be clinging to the ground but in our heart, we have begun the mystical experience of filling a space on this earth with beauty.

Our inner garden has its seasons of planning and creating, too. Often these seasons reflect the changes that come into our life by choice or without warning. We find ourselves facing a new spring - a new beginning - with all its potential. Creating our inner garden in seasons of change requires imagination and courage. We may need to redesign our garden, using a new site and new patterns. We come to understand that we will have many "planting seasons" and without these seasons of change, we cannot create beauty in our lives.

Site

Much thought goes into selecting the right site for our garden. We ponder such things as the sunlight, the shade, protection from wind. Maybe we want to see the garden from a certain window in the house. Perhaps there is an "eye sore" in the yard that we want to improve or even hide! We question whether the site will be accessible to regular care and water. The soil is checked so that we can determine if it will welcome and nourish the seeds and plants.

Our inner gardens require the same thoughtful planning. We come to know that our spiritual growth needs the sunshine of a positive attitude, the protection of prayer and meditation, the nurturing love of good friends and the enriched soil of lessons from past experience.

Connection

When the winter season yields to the warmth of the spring season, we start a close relationship with the plot of ground that we have chosen for our garden site. We examine its boundaries. Will they remain the same or will we change them? The plot is like an old friend who we haven't seen for a long time. We approach hesitantly. The plot is very still, quiet and colorless. We are doing all the talking. It seems that it does not speak to us until we turn that first handful of soil over. Then we make the connection.

After a season of change and loss, we approach our inner garden in much the same manner. We find that our boundaries need to be moved because of the grief experience. Maybe we widen them. As we wander through the garden of our spirit, it seems to be listening to us as though waiting for the plan of new growth. This is a difficult time because we must begin again. We must regain our spiritual strength. We must have faith in the beauty that awaits us. We must connect with our dreams again.

Cultivation

Those first warm days of the planting season are delicious ones. We seem to awaken from a long slumber of inactivity as we push our trowel into the cool soil of the earth. Breaking the soil is a positive sign of the new beginning. A new season has arrived. As we turn the dirt over, we catch the familiar scent of the damp earth with its promise of a haven for the seeds and plants. We stop to break up the clumps with our hands and pull out the weeds that still cling to the soil.

There is nothing more joyful than experiencing the light of hope at the end of that black tunnel of despair. The warmth of those first planting days in our spiritual garden is often beyond expression. We find ourselves taking hold of life again, and our faith has somehow increased tenfold. As we break new soil in our life, we assure the continual growth of our spiritual garden.

Plan

We step back and look at our garden plot with satisfaction after the initial clean-up is over. At this time we firmly shape the plan that we carried in our hearts and minds. We determine the approach we will take to bring about the fullest beauty of the garden. We often reach out to more experienced gardeners for answers. We listen carefully to what worked for them and try out the tips that pertain to our garden.

As we begin to walk out of a crisis, we read other people's stories to find insight into our own experience. We share our experience and receive support from those who have walked through similar troubles in life. We listen carefully to others because spiritual gardens are the same in many ways. We also come to understand that another person's experience does not always pertain to our inner garden's needs. The important thing is that we begin again - that we do not leave our garden without the renewal of love and hope.

Seeding

The planning and preparation of the garden clears the path for bringing the winter dream into the spring of reality. For now it's time to select the seeds and plants that will be put into the soil. We are faced with hundreds of choices! Again we look at our final plan. What will endure the ups and downs of the growing season? What colors will the blossoms bring forth? Which flowers are for show in the garden and which flowers will we bring in as part of a centerpiece or a gift to a friend? Seeding can begin.

Are our spiritual plantings ones that can endure the changes of our emotional climates? Do the blossoms show many colors of understanding, kindness, forgiveness, and selflessness? Which of these inner flowers are for "show" and which ones will become a "routine" in our interaction with others during the day? Which blossoms will we take out of our inner gardens as special gifts for people who need them to replace those that died in their gardens? We pick these flowers, and they grow back tenfold!

Blooming

It doesn't matter what catalogs we memorized during the winter season or what visions of flowers danced in our heads, the surprise of the garden's growth is repeated each spring. We are amazed at first sprouts from the seeds, and enchanted by the first blossom that bursts forth. It remains a mystery to us as this miracle is repeated each season. The mechanics of the garden are easy to understand. The end result fills us with humility as we take a small peek at the power of creation.

Our inner gardens present the same miracles to us as we seek to grow in love and understanding. Often in the midst of a "storm" of hurt and pain, we protect and nourish the seeds of forgiveness and pull out the prickly weeds of hate and resentment. For, we have come to know that forgiveness is a flower that beautifies our inner garden. Hate and resentment grow and kill out the beauty. The end result fills us with humility as we take a small peek at the overwhelming power of love.

Surprise

We enjoy the "little miracles" of our gardens. Sometimes the seeds or plants that we put in our gardens hold little promise in the early growing season. Then, quite unexpectedly, they seem to "take hold" and bloom with incredible beauty and strength. We watch with wonder as they defy all predictions and create a small area of loveliness for all to see and enjoy.

Our inner gardens provide us with many "miracles", too. Often times, the seeds of another person's sharing will unexpectedly burst into bloom during a painful period in our lives. Or a piece of advice that we silently rejected has been seeded and bursts into the bloom of understanding. Every day we find ourselves taking the seeds and plants from our encounters with other people into our inner gardens. Some do not take hold and die, but many bloom where they are planted.

Protection

We step back and view the garden. It has taken on life! The black mounds of dirt hold the promise of the seeds within. The tiny green plants are cuddled in individual "bosoms" of earth. We are filled with the feeling of excitement as we began to visualize the promise of beauty to come. We become very protective and check the soil for moisture. We create shields for the tiny plants which might not withstand the fury of a stormy day. Sometimes we have to replant in areas where plants did not survive that first, fragile growing period. The roots were unable to "take hold". We accept that and begin anew.

Every new inner season offers us another opportunity for spiritual growth. We protect the seeds and plants of new directions and goals. We understand that daily care of prayers, meditation, and spiritual readings keep the soil moist for growth and provide shields for the "stormy days". We view the new season with joy and hope knowing that we will have to work to bring forth the inner blossoms of peace and serenity. Much of the protection and care for the new seeds and plants will come from the support and advice of other "gardeners" in life. We learn that our garden plot is connected to many others in the universe.
We feel strong.

Difference

Our gardens have many different plants. Each has its own special color, appearance and growing cycle. Some flowers bloom early and give us that special early season delight. Others bloom later, and many continue to bloom after the frost has gently put their companions to sleep.

Some plants have a beauty and color that virtually shouts and cannot be missed. Others have a quiet quality with soft shades of color. One needs to look closely and long to discover their special designs and fragile loveliness. They could easily be missed by one who does not come to know every plant in the garden.

We learn through experience to look carefully at what grows in our life's garden. We learn the surprising lesson that the things that shout out and capture our attention can easily overshadow the intricate, lovely small incidents that filter quietly in and out of our day. We learn to be careful so we do not miss the miracles. They enter our lives so quietly.

Weeds

We become frustrated at the weeds that continue to grow in our garden. Time after time we pull them out only to find them growing again. Often in our haste to get a tedious chore done, we pull a weed but do not get the root.

The weeds in our inner garden are perennial fear and anxiety. We are reminded that we need to nourish our garden with trust and faith. We also learn to add a little of the "let go" formula for good measure. We can't ignore the weeds. They have a way of taking over the space needed for the flowers in our life. They strangle the roots of serenity and prevent our inner peace from blossoming. We come to understand that weeds are a part of the bigger picture of our garden. We move into acceptance and keep weeding to make room for the growth in our lives.

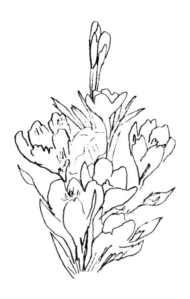

Overcast

Our garden doesn't stop thriving because of overcast weather. In fact, the colors in our garden are always more intense when the light is grey and dim. We seem to pay more attention to every detail and take nothing for granted. We are always touched by the way the wet leaves glisten and straighten up after a rain shower. Everything has that special, fresh look - that "new beginning" look.

We think of the overcast skies that sometimes cover our life's garden in the form of sadness and depression. We wait for the "clearing" and tell ourselves to have faith and "hang on". We draw on strength and courage from past experience and the support of close friends. We come to know we will survive the "downs" and that the "ups" are hidden only by the clouds.

The Storms

Our gardens have survived many storms. Heavy rains, hail and wind have ripped off blossoms and leaves. But, through it all, the roots of the plants often appear to remain intact. Sometimes, we have to spend time firming a root in the ground by adding more soil or by replanting and giving it special thought and attention. Mostly, we watch over the plant until it becomes strong and will thrive on its own.

The storms of our lives sometimes lower our trust level in persons and things. The roots of trust need to be replanted with faith, love and forgiveness. They need to be nurtured carefully and watched with understanding. We know that it is this trust that fosters growth. It helps us to carry on with the knowledge that rainbows appear, and the sun comes out to reflect the brilliant colors of the plants that survived.

Miracle!

There's no special day or time. It just seems to happen. One day you turn the corner into full view of the garden and become overwhelmed with the surprise of its full-grown magnificence. Color radiates from blooming plants and flowers. During those moments, we consciously lock a "memory picture" into our hearts and minds. We look at the once barren plot and are filled with wonder and gratitude. Our faith in the miracles of life is once again renewed.

Often in our life's journey, we live through barren times of emotional pain. We experience hurt, sadness, loss and abandonment. We struggle to nourish the seeds of faith that we plant with empty hearts. Each day we tend the lifeless inner garden which is often watered with our own tears. We tell ourselves to have patience with our grief and wait in pain for a new beginning. Little by little we see the plants of recovery emerge. Our hearts timidly start to sing a quiet song of gratitude as the ache within us grows less. Then, quite unexpectedly, we turn a corner and find our inner garden expressing the miracle of full bloom. We no longer grope for faith but are filled with joy in the knowledge that life holds meaning and purpose again. The miracle has happened!

Harvest

A time comes when the garden has performed most of its miracles of growth and beauty. We gather in the brilliant, fragrant bouquets and fill our surroundings with their loveliness. Some of this harvest is shared with friends. Some is dried and treated for the winter arrangements that keep the summer in our hearts. Other flowers share their beauty with the passers by and gently drop their petals back onto the earth as their time in the garden ends. The harvest time in a garden in a nostalgic one. It is a time of gathering and a time of giving away.

Our inner gardens have many seasons of harvest. We seem to notice these more when a family member or friend comes to us with a barren heart from hurt or loss. It is at these times that we gather in the harvest of our experience in life and give it away. Other times we find ourselves awash in emotional turmoil and find answers in the dried bouquet of our past experiences.

As we gather up each harvest within our inner garden, we find our spiritual strength grows stronger. We come to know that there are always new seasons of planting. We come to have faith in new beginnings. We come to know that each new beginning has the blessings of the many "harvests" of our inner garden. We are at peace.

Virginia Janousek   Water Garden   oil   22x28″

MEDITATIONS in the GARDEN
PART II
Helen Bjornson

words planted on paper
thoughts to grow

I came to gardening late in my life. Though gardening was thrust upon me by circumstances, it quickly lost its "work" status. I easily imagined a new shrub here and a few plants there. Soon the time spent in the garden became a retreat for me, like stepping out of my world for awhile. That was reward enough, so when the garden reached its peak in beauty that first season I could scarcely contain my joy.

Where I'd believed gardening would take too much of my time, I soon realized gardening gave me time. Time to feel my feelings, to ponder, to talk to myself - outloud if I chose, time to plan, to pray - for all those I love and for everything that grows, time to sort it all out. I came to see my life as a garden with seasons and cycles, occasionally pounded by storms, often infested by the pests and noxious plants of the human condition, full of surprises, and always moving toward the Harvest.

Beginning

The beginning of a garden raises questions. There is so much to learn. My inner garden asks if I am ready to grow, willing to do the work, committed to the endeavor? Do I have the endurance to sustain? I know a garden is never "finished", that emotional and spiritual growth go on. My heart cries the answer, "yes"!

I want a plan for my garden, a strategy for success. I research each species and do my best to comply with the directions for healthy growth. I am filled with hope, but I can't completely control what happens in my garden. I can, however, pick my responses to it as I plant seeds of acceptance, flexibility, and openness in my inner garden.

Each Spring the garden makes a new start. Some new occupants, some old, together they blend to complement one another. I make a new start each day. Blending new with old in my inner garden is not always easy. Sometimes I want to shut out what I don't understand. Today I will invite in the unknown, the new, to complement the old.

Site

I view my inner life as a garden to tend, nurture, protect, enrich, enjoy, and move toward Harvest. I tend to my garden daily by making choices, setting priorities, creating healthy boundaries that enhance my life.

✳

My inner life is a garden with the gift of self empowerment . . . . Choice. I choose to grow. I select the time and the place. I direct my growth. I choose to exercise my personal power. The energy, and this dynamism, are as mysterious as seeds bursting beneath the soil.

✳

The site is being chosen now. The joy of the garden won't be delayed until fifteen pounds are lost, the kids are grown, the dog dies, or the sun shines on Thursday. I will live the moment in the garden. I make ready the promise.

✳

I want my garden to thrive, so I choose the site according to the needs of a garden. My inner garden thrives when I choose to be free from the toxic environment of people, systems, and places that inhibit my growth.

Connection

The soil lies still and quiet as though it understands itself and what is to come. It is in quiet and stillness that I come to connect with my inner garden. Allowing time to examine life and to listen to the inner voice helps me to know myself and determine what choices I will make.

The garden changes every day. Even when the plantings look the same as the day before, beneath the soil the roots are taking hold, connecting, growing in strength, giving life. I look to deeper meaning and understanding in my own life. Even when it looks the same as the day before, under the surface my roots are taking hold, connecting, growing in strength.

Gardening is preparing for the coming season, planning, pruning, feeding; a positive experience for a hope-filled future, for Harvest. I am preparing my inner garden in much the same way, planning, praying, nurturing, loving, readying for my Harvest.

Cultivation

I roll up my sleeves and eagerly tackle the task at hand, pulling weeds, digging, and smoothing the soil. I approach it with love and dtermination, knowing that my efforts are worthy, but the outcome belongs to the Master Gardener. My trust is in Him.

＊

This is a beginning, breaking the soil, readying the earth. Out of the dark earth will come new life, rebirth. My inner garden has emerged from darkness to new life, rebirth. It is my comfort to remember this.

＊

Tilling and cultivating are hard work. Hands can blister, muscles ache. The work of my inner garden is difficult, too, as I till the rows of conscience, accountability, and courage.

＊

The garden site must be cultivated. The earth is stirred and broken to be softened. Only then will the soil accept the new seeds or the tender roots. At times in my life I have been broken and softened, until I was finally able to accept seeds of change and new ideas.

Plan

Preparing the soil gives me time to think about my inner garden. Am I seeing and thinking about my life honestly? Am I grateful? Have I said, "I love you"? When did I last help someone? I am preparing the soul, preparing the soil.

✻

The cultivating is finished and I feel good about it. Sweaty, dotted with soil, ready for the garden to begin, I am everyone who has ever dug into their darkness, then raked it smooth.

✻

I cannot anticipate what lies ahead for my garden. For the moment I have the dream and the courage to go forward with it. I am preparing in the best way my knowledge and experience allows. I am open to experiences of others, to ideas, to all the discoveries.

✻

My garden is becoming reality. I contemplate what I wish it to be. I am learning from my inner garden not to seek perfection, for I cannot anticipate the future, but to seek qualities that are important to me and to strive for progress.

Seeding

The seed catalogs arrive while the snow still covers the ground. The promise of Spring sings from their covers. The corners are turned down on favorite pages. The selections are seen in vivid color in the mind's eye and my imagination is in a spin. How lucky I am to be the receiver of the source of certainty that life goes on! The indomitable spirit that houses my inner garden is always singing "Spring". I listen.

Balance is important in the garden. From the Delphinium, tall and stately in the back, to Peony, Sweet William, and Hosta in the front, it's a good plan. I strive for balance in my inner garden. Sometimes I need to redirect energies, even when the plan seems a good one. I long to be able to sway with the breezes that tug me, like the Delphinium.

The Tulip bulbs are planted in bunches. No straight rows for me! My ideas about perfection and "correctness" have been lost in masses of color that cause my spirit to soar. Finally, I understand something the garden is teaching me . . . I love a little mayhem! I give thanks for the gift of wit to enjoy it!

Blooming

A sense of urgency stirs in the back of my mind. It's hard to wait to see the completed project. I hear the voice, "All in good time", I will savor each step of the way, enjoy the process. I will appreciate not only the color, but the stem and leaves and buds and blooms. My inner garden is speaking.

Does a garden become a reflection of its owner? Some gardens are strictly manicured, others flowing and graceful. Still others are allowed to seek their own natural bent. How would I have my garden? Joyful, blossoms sprawling! Inspirational, roses climbing for the sun! Spontaneous, spikes of Iris where least expected! All held solidly together with the deep, soft green of ground cover. Would a friend recognize me?

It was a chance encounter with the Sweet Peas, their purchase motivated by childhood nostalgia. I plopped them against the garage wall. They are thriving, thick and plentiful in blossoms. Their scent is like no other and their presence fills the white wall like paint on an artist's canvas. A chance encounter to marvel at, memories to cherish, enriching the inner garden.

Surprise

It is as though Spring has a delayed action. At first, the sense of it . . . . then anticipation and, finally, the bursting of buds and the long awaited blooms. It is the "newness" that thrills me. Even though I witness the apple blossoms every year, my heart sees them always for the first time. I am filled with the expectations of the fruit. Can I witness life in the same way?

✳

My garden lies beyond the house in the back of the yard, separated from the alley by a tall fence. It can be seen only by invitation through the gate. Few know the secret. When guests come upon it, they are delighted and gaze in astonishment. Oh, that my inner garden could be so rich!

✳

The garden is always a surprise. It is creating itself anew, reaching for its ultimate potential, growing in beauty, strength and grace. It is amazing that it never ceases in its endeavor to fulfill its creation. My inner garden is energized and inspired by its example.

Protection

As I protect the garden, I am reminded to do the same for myself. Worry, obsession, "shoulds", preoccupations, are distractions from which I must protect my inner life. My inner garden teaches me that solutions come from a quiet mind, a listening heart. I keep it simple, stay out of my own way.

The Clematis curls around the base of the Elm, their paths crossing unexpectedly as paths have crossed mine. Paths of people who have protected me, helped me, sustained and supported me, shared their lives, created and completed Harvests in the inner garden with me. For strangers and friends, I am praying my thanks.

Stakes support the taller plants. Winds and rains could beat them down without defense for their roots. I am staking my inner garden with solitude, meditation, and prayer.

Difference

The garden makes room for new growth. Thriving on variety, unafraid of the new and different, it expands its boundaries to encompass all and flourishes. I am learning by the garden's example to welcome variety, challenge my fear of the new and different, and expand my boundaries.

The flowers reach their fulfillment in their own time, unconcerned with the progress of one another. So it must be with me. Comparison with others stunts my growth. It, too, will be fulfilled in its own time. I am growing in patience.

Roses make a dramatic presentation, climbing strong on the arbor. They catch my full attention. As I look closely, I notice Baby's Breath, quietly supporting the roses, giving itself entirely to the task. Loving is like that. Oh, that I will grow enough to give myself entirely to such a task; as supportive in love as the Baby's Breath.

The ground cover blossoms, adding brilliance to its soft, dependable display. It seems small, almost insignificant, yet it holds the entire garden in its perimeter like the quiet experiences that hold a life. I am coming to appreciate and value quiet times.

Weeds

Weeds are a part of gardening requiring preventive methods. Prevention is an answer for weeds in my inner garden as well. Through daily examination of conscience, meditating, journaling, sharing with friends, I am learning to know a weed when I see one.

✳

Weeds are familiar to me. I've pulled them before; dandelions of doubt, thistles of rage, nettles of self pity, cockleburs of shame. I feel sure I have the root, but it surprises me and reappears! I keep pulling! I am stronger than the weed.

✳

There are days when I feel like a weed. My mind sprouts negative messages; too slow, too fat, too short, too old. If I am not watching, negativity will take over my personality like crabgrass in a neglected garden. I stand ready, trowel in hand.

✳

There is a weed in my garden that looks as lovely as any flower, until its thistles appear. I let it stay because it cautions me to look deeply and honestly beneath the surface of my life.

Overcast

The garden is the same, whether the sky is clear or not. It endures, rises to the occasion, holds steadfast. I am longing to be so rooted.

✳

The clouds cover the earth. The garden appears at rest. I am resting, collecting thoughts, making plans, snuggling under the cover, and finding the peace of my inner garden.

✳

The garden cannot choose its sky, nor can I. But I can choose my response to it. From my inner garden, I choose my attitude and mood to be positive and grateful.

✳

An overcast is acceptable to the garden. Not knowing, not being sure of what will happen next is part of the growing process of my inner garden. I cannot control the weather, but I am sowing an attitude of trust.

Storms

Storms can come to the garden unexpectedly. Am I a storm, lashing out in sarcasm or criticism in my own garden or the gardens of others?

The run-off from the rain storm leaves deep trenches in the ground. In time these will be filled by new soil. As for my inner garden, the new soil of fresh ideas, positive attitudes, habits for healthy growth will fill the deep trenches of loss and repair torn roots.

There is work to done to repair the garden after a damaging storm. I gather broken branches, secure stakes, and shelter the wounded growth. My inner garden has been lashed by storms of addiction, depression, broken relationships, shattered dreams. To repair, I am claiming my brokenness, sheltering my wounds with prayer, securing the inner garden with the healing power of sharing in trust.

The rainbow reconnects the earth to the sky, making amends following the storm. It offers brilliant colors of peace and promise for my garden. I am choosing to be a rainbow. I am choosing to make amends.

Miracle

The Day Lily has one bright, shining moment. One day to show its exquisite bloom. As the gardener I stay alert so as not to miss any moment of its beauty. To be aware of the beauty of the moment, to be fully in the NOW, to be present in my own inner garden, is to be free to witness miracles.

I love the garden and the gardening process. It enriches me. I am grateful for the miracle of growth, humbled by the beauty that rose from my plot of empty soil. I am aware of the Power greater than myself. I can only guess what such a Power has in store for me.

To see a rose in perfect bloom takes my breath away. How could it be perfect? I don't really know what perfection is, but I recognize this as a miracle, without comparison. I am finding my own perfection within my inner garden. Comparisons to others' talents prevent miracles. The rose knows this. I am learning.

Harvest

My inner life reflects the gardening process of preparing cultivating, blooming, dying, harvesting. I experience transitions in this life garden that I see now as Harvests. Some years the yields are high, some I tally losses, but always the beauty has been abundant. May I grow through the years with the grace of my garden.

Some color remains in the garden, brilliant as when new. Stems have turned dark telling me their energies have gone back to their roots. I am salvaging the remaining flowers, treasuring them the most because they are the last. I want to hold the miracle longer, even as the cycle begins again.

In this garden season, once again, a plot of soil becomes my teacher. The experience, the process, turned inward, gives me confidence that growth is ongoing, that my inner garden benefits from care, nuturing, hard work. It experiences storms and grows through them. It will bear fruits of love and reach Harvests over and over again. I am a miracle.

We are grateful to:

Virginia Janousek, well known artist, whose
paintings are reproduced in this book

Ann C. Kavanaugh, Ph.D. and
Glenna Henderson for their editing skills

James O'Rourke for his design ideas reflected
in the book's format.

The Associated Arts staff of Moorhead,
Minnesota, for their patience and guidance
during both the first and second printings of
"The Garden".

Our families and friends who led us to believe
that this book was a necessary point in our
life's journey.

. . . and to the spirit that speaks within each of
us. We are grateful.

The Seventh Elm
P.O. Box 2905 Fargo, ND
58108